PROSTITUTE

TO

PROFESSOR

A Guide To Radical Transformation

Becca Jacobson MA, M.Ed

"You are not the same person
that you were in the past"

~Dr. Ben Hardy

Copyright © 2024

All Rights Reserved

Dedication

To every human who ever struggled, failed, and struggled again.

Contents

Dedication iii

Introduction vi

The Family Business 1

The White Pants 6

Motherly Advice 11

    Take-Away: Shame & Self-Reproach 15

        Coaching Call! Sacred Space 22

        Your Personal Invitation 24

Go ahead and Jump 26

Kindergarten Lessons 30

Father/Daughter Lessons 34

    Take-Away: The Joke's On Us 40

        Coaching Call! Your Journal 45

The Black Out 49

The Laughter 55

Cocaine Man vs. The Redneck 59

    Take-Away: Carrying Others' Words 64

        Coaching Call! Journaling Opportunity 69

The Killer Couch 72

The Convenient Death 76

The Valium Years 82

    Take-Away: Self-sabotage 87

        Coaching Call! Find your Tribe Today 92

The Bathtub Murder 93

Mother/Daughter Lessons 97

The Sober Sunrise 101

    Take Away: How to Transform 106

        Coaching Call! Get your community now 110

Resources 111

About The Author 112

Introduction

This book is about personal transformation: yours and mine. In it I share my memoirs to show you that it doesn't matter where we're coming from, we can reinvent ourselves. These are stories of how I went from an addicted, alcoholic prostitute living in isolation and loneliness to an addicted, alcoholic professor living in isolation and loneliness, to a happy, growing human. There are stories in this book of violence and sex and drugs and despair, and they're all true. I lived them and have finally gleaned from them the lessons I was meant to learn. But we don't have to come from such a drastic background to want change and growth in life. Indeed, change and growth are what we're here for. Every challenge we face is put there to teach us something, and if we take a victim stance, we learn nothing.

I was a prostitute in the true sense of the word, but the fact is that many people are selling their lives to mediocrity because of busyness, fear, lack of confidence, complacency, and a host of other reasons. And let's not forget our myriad "harmless" addictions like social media, sugar, food, sex and almost anything else the human mind decides to grab onto. I hope that by now we all know that anything we do to excess holds us back from our potential.

But I have discovered that it doesn't have to be that way. We can live as many lives as we want. We can seize our lives, take control of them, truly live them. It doesn't matter where you are now or where you've been. It doesn't matter if you want a completely different life or simply some key changes in your basic habits and routines; either way, you can have it.

These stories turned out to be tougher to write than I thought, shocking even, when I saw them all together, but I'm glad I've done it. They're all mine. They represent a significant part of my life, and until this moment, I've kept them hidden except for fragments. And I'm sharing them now to show you that change is possible and nothing is unforgivable.

If you are a person who knows, in the depths of your being, that you were meant to rise above the ordinary, then we've got something in common and I'm glad you're with me on this journey. The fact is that there is no ordinary human and we deserve to live the lives we want. We don't have to conquer the world to live our best lives, we just need to know what we want and take the actions that will get us there.

In this book, I will tell you 13 stories and share with you some keys to change that I have discovered. You'll learn how I broke free, but, more importantly, we'll look at some of the beliefs and mindsets that keep us from realizing our true potential. They're lies we tell ourselves, they're lies that society tells us, they're weaknesses that leave us wide open to obsessions like sugar, social media, shopping, food and sex and they keep us shackled to mediocrity. Sometimes they're so subtle that we live with them and don't even notice that they're damaging our lives, our health, our relationships, our emotional health, our mental health, our happiness and our chance to live a free and joyous life. In fact, they even try to tell us that living a "free and joyous life" isn't part of the human condition.

This book is a powerful tool specifically designed to be used in combination with an open heart and mind, a journal, and the willingness to both reflect and take action.

I'm sending this book out into the world to find you because I want you to wake up and seize your life. If you're shackled to anything that keeps you from experiencing the freedom and joy that is your birthright as a human, then keep on reading and take action. If you experience regret or shame about anything you've done or experienced in the past, then follow my lead.

We can learn self-love. We can live in this world with our heads held high. How do I know? Because I've done it, I've studied and practiced the pathways to freedom, and I've helped others to set themselves free. And I've also done a lot that one might otherwise assume I should be ashamed of. I used to be ashamed and shackled, but I'm not anymore. And if I can let go of my past and my resentments of myself and others and learn self-love, then so can you. Personal growth is a life-long journey. We are all works in progress.

My ultimate message is that if we want to, we can transform our lives. We must ditch the comfort zone and grow. We can live free from compulsive behaviors that are actually humiliating to humans whose birthright includes the freedom to choose our own thoughts and actions. To be compelled by habit to act against our own best interest is not only humiliating to the human spirit, it's beneath our dignity. And if we've behaved in ways in the past that have led us to regret, we can learn to let them go, no matter what demons lurk there.

So welcome to your transformation guide, my friend. This is your wake-up call, should you choose to hear it, and I offer it to you with love.

The Family Business

In my early 20's, I found myself in a hotel room where a "stag party" was happening. I was one of only two women present: we were the entertainment that night. The room was full of young men celebrating the upcoming wedding of one of them and they'd called a local escort service to get a couple of "those women" to come to the hotel and offer up entertainment. We were expected to dance, tease, you know, entertain.

And that's exactly what I did. The hotel suite had two rooms, the second one was a space for any of the men who wanted something extra and were willing to pay for it. I found myself in that room four times that night. I'd come back out, dance around for a while, then get led back into the separate room by a different young man and so it went into the wee hours. As the night progressed, I struggled to keep my drinking under control because it would be dangerous to lose my wits. But, I'd done this before and knew how to look after myself. Beside, me and the other woman there had a "protector" outside waiting in the parking lot whose job it was to make sure we came out safely by 2am. If we didn't he would come and knock on the door. There were no cell phones then, but we all had pagers that we could call as long as we could access a phone.

All was well.

That night I made $2700 and spent time 1:1 with four men while entertaining the whole group in between. The woman with me made about the same. Her name was "Jessica" on nights like this, but her real name, for me, was "mom." And the man in the parking lot was "step dad."

My mom was a business woman. She opened "Gentlemen's Escorts" and I worked for her now and then when I was in town. At the time of this party, she was 46 and I was 21. We made a pretty good team. Gentlemen's Escorts was a thriving business and my mom was a serious business woman. She kept strict books and had developed standard operating procedures along the way. She was a tough-minded woman who took control of anyone and anything around her. Her husband, who had been my step dad since I was 10, followed along with her: he knew he couldn't stop her from doing anything once she had made up her mind to do it.

And in her early 40's she made up her mind. She had worked her whole life for barely more than minimum wage. She was uneducated, suffered from undiagnosed and untreated emotional and mental disorders (such as addiction, depression and bi-polar disorder) her whole life but didn't realize it or wouldn't acknowledge it. She was a survivor of the highest sort: when she got an idea, nothing would stop her from making it happen. So, at 41, she decided it was time to get a tidy retirement fund together and to hell with society, to hell with working for others, to hell with what others thought. She put an ad in the paper inviting men to call. And she wasn't about to put up with violence or abuse of any kind. She called her business "Gentlemen's" for a reason. In the beginning, at the time of this party, she took a lot of calls that she would later say no to, but at this point, she was still building the business. Her business model was clear: establish a stable of customers that were married professionals and serve them regularly over time. At this time, I was living in a different city, and had established myself in the world of exotic dancing. And when I went to visit, the inevitable happened: I went on some calls for my mom's business because when the call was from a young man, she knew that they would likely be disappointed to have a 40+ woman show up. At first, she objected to me working for her, but she knew I was working anyway, and since I was usually broke, she let me go on a few calls.

So, in the early years, I worked for her now and then, but it didn't take long for her plan to materialize. She got her 10-12 regulars and shut down the ads. This group of mature, professional family men, who did not know each other of course, were sufficient for her to build her retirement nest egg. Each one had a schedule, some saw her every couple of weeks, others once a month. And, of course, relationships were formed. My mom became a listener, the sex was secondary and sometimes not what they wanted or needed. They talked about things they knew would go nowhere else. They were safe with her and she treated them like kings for an hour or two and they went away feeling refreshed, heard, and ready to face their lives again. One of the men was a local celebrity, another a professor, there was a logger, a banker, and so on. Most of them were family men. All were respectful and treated my mom like a dear friend. At least one left everything in his estate to my mom.

I was able to get to a point, in my mid 30's, of feeling acceptance and respect for my mom after spending my teens and twenties in resentment. I was somehow gifted the ability to let these go and build a relationship with her before she died. I had been searching for a way to a better life. I had taken some meditation classes, read some spiritual books, and enough had rubbed off that I was able to reframe my relationship with her and my past, even though I'd never heard the term, "reframe."

I reasoned: She did not know how to parent children. How could she? No one ever taught her about acceptance or forgiveness, which are the two keys to my freedom today. I accept the past, I forgive myself and others. She never learned. She took her resentments, her sadness, her fears, her judgment and her broken heart, to her grave, but she had bigger balls than a lot of men I've known and I loved her dearly all the days of her life.

But that's another story…

Becca Jacobson MA, M.Ed.

The White Pants

When I was 15, I was no longer living with my mom. We just couldn't get along. But I stayed in school and I knew I had to work, so I got a job as a waitress in a family restaurant. I learned a ton! I was a good waitress. I learned how to treat customers, handle money, show up on time, and work with others. I really was good at it, and I worked hard because I wanted the tips.

After I had been there a few months, some of the waitress's

tip money started going missing. We would each have a cup with our name on it and when someone left us a tip on the table, we put it in the waitress's cup. Well, one day, we realized that money from our cups was disappearing. For example, one day, I saw my customer leave me a one-dollar bill, but I was serving someone else and couldn't pick it up. And later that day, it never appeared in my cup. This was frustrating and it also made me sad to think that someone I worked with would take my money. Everyone seemed so nice and I was beginning to think of them all as friends. But I was sure that the boss would do something about it, so I just did my work. I was becoming pretty friendly with the other waitresses, the cook and my boss and I felt like I was fitting in. I always liked to fit in and I liked to do things properly, to learn and become accomplished in my work.

One day one of the regular customers, a man about 30, asked me to go out with him and I didn't want to because he was so old. I asked one of the older waitresses what I should do and she gave me this advice. "Tell him you're flattered, thank him for asking, and say no". It kinda shocked me because it was so different from anything my mom might have said. She would have sneered, laughed, and told me he was only after one thing. But when I thought about it, I realized that I was flattered, and I was glad, so I went ahead and said in my best grown-up voice, "I'm flattered, but I can't go out with you right now." Those words, "I'm flattered" were so foreign to me.

I understood that I was making him feel okay for asking, I was saying those words to make sure not to hurt his feelings, but I never would have thought of saying them on my own. They just weren't the kinds of words I'd ever heard anyone in my family use. And it worked, he smiled and said, "Maybe another time." It felt really good to have a mother figure advising me; I had never experienced that and I really started feeling like I had found somewhere safe.

Our uniforms were a yellow and white waitresses' top supplied by the restaurant, and we were supposed to wear white pants with it that we supplied ourselves. I was still really skinny and I had no white pants that fit me right. The ones I was wearing were baggy and unflattering. But I couldn't afford to buy new ones. For a few weeks, I kept thinking about how it would feel to have nice white pants, you know, denim ones that fit me right, maybe with pockets in the front. One of the other girls wore those and they looked really good. I had never had nice clothes. I'd never been able to dress like the other kids. I wanted white pants that were flattering. I became obsessed.

Then one day before work, I went to the mall to a clothing store. They had the exact pants I wanted, but I knew I couldn't afford them. I wanted them *so bad*. I went into the change room with a bunch of stuff, put the pants in my bag, held my breath and began to walk out of the store. I thought my heart would burst and I could feel the back of my neck tingling as I slowly crossed the threshold of the store to go out into the mall.

Sure enough, I felt my arm being grabbed and the woman from the store spun me around. I was doomed. I was humiliated. I was so wracked with shame in that moment I felt I would give anything to just turn back the clock for 5 minutes and be free from this horrible, mortifying scene.

It turned out that the owner of the store was friends with the owner of the restaurant. Her first call was to tell my boss that they had caught me stealing. They didn't call the police; instead, I was told to report to the restaurant the next day. All night, I fretted, worried, and cried. I had no one to talk to about this. And even if I did, I would be too ashamed to tell them. Over the last few months, the only people in my life were the other waitresses and my boss, and most of them treated me like a little sister. And now I had let them all down. I hoped and prayed that night that they would forgive me. I hoped they would give me grace because I hadn't stolen something frivolous. The pants, after all, were for work, and I really didn't have enough money to buy new ones. My wages were $3.50 an hour (minimum wage), and I paid room and board with a married couple while attending high school on the days I didn't skip classes to take a shift at the restaurant. I was trying hard to be grown up, independent and figure out how to make money in life because it was my number one, one and only goal and it always had been. My mom taught me well: "You need money or life isn't worth living!"

The next day, I was not only immediately fired by my boss but I was given silent glares by everyone in the restaurant, even the regular customers. I expected that, but I was astonished to hear that it wasn't because I'd stolen the pants, they said, but because I had been stealing tips from my fellow waitresses all this time.

Speechless.

Later, I would think about that scene and wonder which one of them was the real thief. Did she stop taking the tips after I left? If she was smart, she would have, but I've since learned that thieves like that rarely reform. She's a real thief. A person who plans and takes things from people who trust her. She does it day in and day out and that kind of dishonesty is hard to change. On the other hand, I haven't picked up anything that didn't belong to me from that day to this, so I guess it was a good lesson learned.

But, I was too young and ignorant to know how important it is not to let resentment, cynicism and self-pity rule our lives. I was angry. I had been wronged and the world owed me an apology. I was a victim. And since I couldn't seem to do anything about it in the external world, I started saying yes to the joints that were offered at lunch during school and the beer that was floating around at night. Why not? I figured that the world wasn't fair and I would show them a thing or two: I would get loaded!

Sweet revenge.

And, of course, I was now unemployed. It would take about two years, but I would get another job and it would be one that paid a lot more money.

But that's another story…

Motherly Advice

My first husband loved to tell jokes like this one: "What's the difference between a virgin and a toilet?... The toilet doesn't follow you around after you use it." This "joke" reminds me of a weekend in 1977 when I was 12.

I was a flat-chested, skinny kid. My sister, on the other hand, wow! She wore a bra! And she had boys hanging around her. I followed her around like a toilet, just wanting to be a part of her world, hoping some of it would rub off. She was doing things! Like smoking pot and kissing boys and who knows what else. I stared wide-eyed at her. I wondered incessantly what it was like to be noticed.

One particular weekend, my sister's boyfriend was staying at our house. I don't remember how she talked Mom into that, but that was my sister: she could do things I would never figure out in a million years. So, my 14-year-old sister's 17-year-old boyfriend was staying at our house for the weekend, and I tried to just be near them, hoping some of their "cool" would rub off. I lingered, I loitered. I was a little lost lamb. She would tell me to buzz off, but I would casually wander into the rec room in the basement where they were hanging out and try to be invisible. I heard her say things like, "Once you know how to tickle their balls, they're yours for life." What does that mean?! I was so shocked, I guess it showed on my face because my sister and her boyfriend burst out laughing at me. I was so uncool. I slithered away.

Later that day, after dinner, my sister's boyfriend walked past me and whispered, "You should come to my room tonight." I was so shocked I couldn't breathe. "Was he serious?" "What did he want with me?" I was so excited. Something was finally happening in my life. I felt like someone for the first time in my life. Something was happening! I went to bed early and lay there staring at the ceiling until the house was silent. Then I got out of bed, tiptoed to the spare room downstairs and quietly opened the door. He was sleeping on a cot and immediately said, "Come here, Becky." He knew my name! Just hearing it come out of his mouth made me feel so important. I existed!

I moved toward the cot, and he grabbed me, threw me on it, hopped on top of me, lifted my nighty, shoved himself inside me, and then rolled off and said, "Go back to bed."

I went.

What happened? Did I do something wrong? I was bewildered. As I made my way back to my room, I realized I was wet and stinging between the legs. I laid in my bed, about 5 minutes had passed and I was staring at the same ceiling, but I was not the same girl. I had a boyfriend! Surely tomorrow he would talk to me, let me hang out, be nice to me! I was so excited. I was somebody. I was as good as my sister.

My sister's boyfriend left the next day without a glance in my direction, and we never saw him again. I was itchy between the legs in the days following his visit and it grew worse with each passing day. I was terrified. I didn't know what to do. On the fourth day, I had no choice. I needed help. I approached my mom's room. She was sitting up in bed with her crochet and a cup of tea. I peered into her room, "Mom?"

"What do you want?" she asked, looking exhausted. As I somehow croaked out the words, explaining my problem, I watched her face contort with disgust and rage, and when I was done, she ground her teeth together, squinted at me with loathing, and very quietly, very slowly, whispered, "you. little. slut."

And I was. She was right, of course. And I would spend the next few decades living up to her expectations.

But that's another story…

Take-Away: Shame & Self-Reproach

"Shame loves secrecy. The most dangerous thing to do after a shaming experience is hide or bury our story. When we bury our story, the shame metastasizes."

–Brené Brown-

As my stories unfold in this book, it will become clear to you why I ended up burying my head in shame. I'm starting with this take-away because it's what kept me hostage for over 3 decades: shame leads to isolation, which ensures we'll never grow. A powerful trap. You don't have to have a drastic past like mine to feel shame; many people deal out self-reproach as though it was a necessary part of life as they hold on to some "dirty little secret" they believe is unforgivable. I want you to know, there's no such thing as unforgivable.

Becca Jacobson MA, M.Ed.

While guilt can be healthy and spur us to better behavior in the future, extended self-reproach and feelings of shame are major blocks to growth and happiness. You can overcome shame about your past in a heartbeat or it could take time, but you can do it and I'm going to show you why you should and how you can begin today.

To begin with, extended self-reproach becomes self-indulgent. Yup, I said it. If we're not careful, having something to feel bad about becomes a perverted form of enjoyment. I ought to know, I wallowed around in this for years that could have been spent living. I thought that the things I had done were unforgivable, that I was beyond redemption. I will admit that my actions were questionable, but they were not unforgivable. Some may choose to judge, and that's they're baggage. I see so clearly the profound impact that self-forgiveness can have on one's well-being. The fact is that I lived most of my life in intense shame and I tried to drown it with drugs and alcohol or by trying to ignore it entirely, but until I faced the past, spit it all out, looked at it, it was there in the background like the proverbial elephant in the room, except I was the only one who knew it was there. In fact, as I write these words, I have only experienced 5 years of freedom from the cancerous states of regret and shame. That's too long to wait.

My life is punctuated throughout by time that could have been spent doing so many things other than drinking and feeling bad about myself. What about yours? We don't have to be a prostitute or an addict or a thief to feel shame. It comes in many forms. Are you allowing your past actions to steal your life today? I urge you to find it within yourself to refuse to use one more moment of your life in shame and guilt. We can and must learn to love ourselves.

Shame is a toxic, pervasive emotion that can entrench us in a cycle of self-destructive behaviors. Shame will keep us stuck. Unsurprisingly, we know that there's a strong correlation between shame and substance use.

Learning to forgive ourselves disrupts this cycle of shame. By acknowledging our mistakes, taking responsibility, and extending compassion to ourselves, we dismantle the foundations upon which shame thrives. The process of self-forgiveness becomes a powerful tool in breaking free from the shackles of living life like an automaton, refusing to face the underlying feelings and instead numbing ourselves with whatever offers relief. It doesn't matter what you choose to use, attempting to hide will only make your underlying feeling worse until you live every day of your life…unhappy. Even if you never hit some horrible bottom, even if you're not drinking or doing drugs, if you're numbing out in any way, refusing to face your feelings of low self-worth, you will at the very least end up just plain unhappy.

Also, let me gently point out that those of us who dwell endlessly on how bad we are invariably become incredible bores to other people. The world loses interest very quickly. We've got to take responsibility so we can be of cheerful service to others. Nothing, and I mean nothing, that you've done in the past disqualifies you from living free and at peace with yourself. If you owe an apology, do it and move on. You are not a martyr.

Central to the concept of self-forgiveness is the practice of self-compassion. We must treat ourselves with the same kindness and understanding we would offer to a friend. Individuals who practice self-compassion experience lower levels of anxiety and depression. This underscores the importance of incorporating self-compassion into the process of self-forgiveness, offering a practical approach for us as we choose to let go and move forward.

And it's not just about us. As someone who believes in the transformative power of community, I believe that it's crucial to recognize the ripple effect that self-forgiveness can have on the collective healing of a group. When individuals within a community learn to forgive themselves, they contribute to the creation of a culture of empathy and understanding.

We must embrace the reality of human imperfection and extend this to ourselves. The path to freedom is not linear, and setbacks are an inherent part of the process. Research in the field of positive psychology emphasizes the importance of adopting a growth mindset, wherein challenges are viewed as opportunities for learning and development. Learning to forgive ourselves aligns with this growth-oriented perspective. By shedding the burden of perfectionism and embracing the lessons embedded in our mistakes, we pave the way for sustained and meaningful transformation.

Here's the powerful truth that I'm asking you to embrace: the past is not a prison; it's a launchpad. We have the power to rewrite our stories, to infuse them with meaning and purpose, and to use them as catalysts for positive change. Remember, it's not about erasing the past; it's about reframing it and imbuing it with a sense of purpose and gratitude that propels us forward. It's about accepting ourselves, warts and all. As you read my stories, you will see me doing this. You'll see me reframing my relationship with my mom and others. And, most importantly, with myself. Watch for it. Take note. Apply what you notice.

Take out your journal and write one story that you'd rather forget because it brings you shame. Remember it in detail, and allow yourself to feel the pain of remorse. Then look at it from an outsider's perspective. If your daughter came to you with this story, would you shame her? What about your best friend? Would you reject her, shame her, make her suffer for years?

Of course not! So I ask: do you not deserve the same compassion?

Write this down: I'm human, and I made a mistake, just like every other human. I forgive myself. I love myself.

And when I say, "like every other human," I mean it. Let's use my first story, "The Family Business," as an example. Who should be feeling shame in this story? Me? My Mom? The young man who decided to engage in sex on the night before his wedding? The other young men who were there and also in relationships? Or what about those clients my mom had? As I said, they were all professional (that is, socially respectable) family men. Who's to blame in this story? Where does the shame lie?

How we answer these questions will vary, of course, depending on our outlook on life. And, the truth is, that the answers don't matter. What matters is the take-away for you and me today: we're all infallible. You would be very surprised to know some of the secrets those around you carry. Does it matter?

No. It doesn't matter. Each of us needs to answer to ourselves. Each of us needs to learn to live with ourselves and the choices we've made. We're not inherently bad. As we've said, we're human and we make mistakes. We act from impulse, and we often make choices that are not in our highest interest. We act to satisfy a craving, or to get a thrill, knowing that we are likely to regret it later. Whether or not we learn to resist these urges is a personal journey each of us must attend to alone or with our God.

But this I do know: passing judgment on ourselves or others is not our job. Most of us will agree that we shouldn't judge others, but I want you to notice that I included you in that statement. You don't get to pass judgment on yourself. No, you don't. We think we can, we think we deserve to be punished. N. O.

    Whatever it is, join me, my friend, and transform your life.

Coaching Call! Sacred Space

How seriously do you take your personal development? I believe that our growth, until we take our last breath, is the reason we're here. If we're not growing, we're going backwards. There is no standing still. Have you noticed how we have a space in our homes to feed and clean and rest the body, but most of us don't have a space for personal growth? It's time to prioritize.

If you don't already have one, I invite you to create a space for study and growth. This is your space. Let's call it your sacred space. The term "sacred" generally refers to something regarded with reverence and respect, and although often associated with divinity, religious beliefs, or spiritual significance, this is not necessarily that case. We're using the word to underscore the idea to ourselves that this goes beyond the realm of the ordinary and is considered set apart, inviolable. Your growth matters. We are willing to take time to make sure our bodies are healthy, our bank accounts are healthy, what about our emotional/mental/spiritual selves?

So, this is your assignment: a personal, sacred space for reflection, change, peace, and personal rejuvenation. This is a space that makes you feel good. It's peaceful, you should like the smell there, you are comfortable and warm and safe there. And others know that it's your space and it deserves to be respected. Using the same space for study, prayer, meditation, relaxation, will build up energy in that space and your subconscious soon realizes, as you enter the space, that it's time for your personal growth and rejuvenation and change.

Let me share mine with you as an example. It's a spare room in our house, which could have been for guests, but I claimed it as my own. In this room I have pictures of people and places that inspire me. I have incense, candles, a yoga mat, books, cushions and a custom-sized meditation bench that my husband made for me with his own hands out of beautiful recycled fir. In this room, no shoes are allowed, not even house slippers. I consider this a sacred space and it says to my subconscious: "I am worthy. I matter. My internal life is important. I will give myself the gift of time, a little bit each day will do, and I will sit quietly, pray, meditate, read, write, stretch the body and fortify my soul before going out into the world to be of service."

Now it's your turn. If you can't find a room all for yourself, it doesn't matter, a corner of a room, a particular chair, somewhere that you can call your own, will do. In this space I want you to begin a simple daily ritual that tells your subconscious, "I matter. I am worthy." Try to go to your space each day at the same time, go with intention. Ideally, you'll go there twice each day: in the morning before the world barges into your consciousness and in the evening before you turn in. In fact, if I can convince you to incorporate that one habit into your life, I'll be happy. Even 5 minutes each morning and evening will begin to change your life.

Go there to read this book and use your journal. I will show you how. Go quietly and humbly and give yourself the gift of remembering that you're not a bag of flesh and bones, but a beautiful, glowing spirit that deserves love, respect, compassion, and care. Each and every day. And once you've replenished yourself, you'll be better equipped to grow the life you crave while also being of service to the world, knowing that our rewards in life are directly related to our service to others. This is not a selfish practice!

Your Personal Invitation

If you are a person who loves self-help but has struggled in the past to get the promised results, then you are invited to join us at the *We Transform Together Academy* where we read, discuss and implement (*action is our watch-word!*) some of the best self-help books ever written. There we all have a common goal: to grow, to make sure we're moving forward and finally getting rid of that feeling of frustration that comes when we try alone and don't get results. That is such a common feeling that I decided to do something about it because the solution is so simple: do it together!

You'll find others like you, you'll find resources I've created, such as access to previous book studies, journal prompts, success checklists, videos discussing the secrets to successful implementation, change, follow through and much more. The whole philosophy of the academy is to support one another and reap the rewards we crave, regardless of what our goals are. As we enthusiastically go through our favorite books, we're improving our health, losing weight, getting a handle on our finances, upleveling our relationships, getting the careers we want and much more. You can share this invitation with someone you love and give them a gift of transformation.

But be warned! This is not a community of dabblers; it is not your grandmothers' book club. We are taking action and getting results.

You are invited.

https://go.wetransformtogether.com/community

Go ahead and Jump

I arrived in Calgary late on a Sunday night in 1986 and they gave me a room on the 8th floor. The city was quiet. I was working at the hotel's club for the week and was settling in when a knock came to my door. I opened it and there stood Michael, a DJ from one of the other clubs that I'd been hanging out with for a few months. He was starting to bug me and I wasn't thrilled to see him. "What are you doing here?" I asked.

"Rebecca, I can't stand it anymore. Let's get out of this life, go away together and start something normal. Let's get out of here. I want you".

"No," I said.

He continued for about 20 minutes trying to convince me to change my mind but there was no way I was going with him anywhere. If that was ever going to happen, it wouldn't be with him. He just wasn't the guy, and I knew it.

He begged some more, and I was getting tired of it. He stood in the middle of the room facing me, while I stood facing him with the window a few feet behind me. Finally, he said, "Is that your final decision?"

"Yes," I said, and he quickly strode toward me. Oh crap, I thought, he's getting violent. I stood aside to get out of his way, but he just strode right past me, and I heard glass breaking behind me.

"Shit!" I thought, he's broken the hotel's window and I'm going to have to pay for it. The room was quiet as I stood there for a couple of moments. Finally, I turned around and was shocked to see that I was alone in the room. A winter breeze gently moved the curtain through the broken window, but Michael was not there. I was so shocked that I couldn't understand what had happened, and then it hit me.

I ran to the window, looked out and there he was, laying on the street in downtown Calgary, 8 floors below.

I ran to the door, down 8 flights of stairs, past the front desk, yelling, "Call an ambulance!" and out the front doors. It was Sunday evening and the street was very quiet. Michael's body was in the strangest position. I approached him and sat on the curb. He turned his head and looked at me. I couldn't believe that he was alive. He said he loved me. He hadn't said that before tonight. Then people arrived and I was pushed away. The police took me to my room to look at the window and ask me a bunch of questions. I guess they wanted to make sure I hadn't thrown the 6'1" Michael out the window. Everything was a blur.

Michael's body was sent home the next day to his parents on the East Coast. He was 22.

When I went back to the club where he had worked, everyone wanted to know what happened. I was a sort of celebrity for a while. I got a lot of drinks bought for me and I told the story over and over. I got comments like, "wow, remind me not to get mixed up with you, it's deadly!" or "who knew you were so amazing men jump to their deaths over you!" And the other DJ, who had worked with Michael, took a moment out between strippers to do a tribute.

Over the mic, he announced, "Everyone, this song is for Micheal," and he played Van Halen's hit song from a few years earlier. The song was called, "Jump."

As the music blasted through the dark, smokey bar, I looked

around and saw young men sitting at the edge of the stage, ("gynecology row," they called it), laughing, yelling at each other over the music, drinking their beer and waiting for the next dancer. These were hard-working men, mostly from the oil rigs, who would marry, have kids, live ordinary lives while getting the odd thrill at the local strip club. At the back of the room, deep in the dark recesses, sat the bikers, all proudly wearing the patches they had earned, apparently symbols of their loyalty and toughness. Unlike the others, they sat seriously, leaning in to share secrets with each other and staying aloof. With them sat a few of the other dancers with big, crunchy hair, 5-inch heels, all legs, lips and cleavage, making themselves available. The regulars, wrinkled and graying, sat at the bar, lined up like birds on a wire, ignoring everything except the glasses in front of them. The DJ booth was in the center of the room, lit up with flashing red and blue lights. The smoke was thick; the atmosphere felt so heavy I could hardly breath, despite everyone's attempt at "partying."

As the lyrics hit me, "go ahead and jump," I suddenly felt deep sadness, remorse, and shame trying to wash over me, so I resolutely renewed my commitment to my drink, my forgetting, my escape.

It wouldn't be until 2018, 32 years later, that I would finally stop running for good.

But that's another story…

Kindergarten Lessons

When I was under 10, I still believed that I would be loved and safe if I obeyed my mom and teachers and tried my hardest. If I succeeded I would be loved. And because of that I had a deep respect for my teachers and any authority figure. One day when I was about 5, the teacher had an amazing new activity for us.

"Today we're going to play a game and pretend that we live on an exotic island with palm trees and endless sunshine. We are natives from the past and we have a queen who rules our land.

To show the queen our love, each day we give her great love and praise in our native language. And I'm going to teach you a bit of that exotic language"

I was so excited! I was going to learn a new language. With a fierce determination to get this right, I listened intently as the teacher continued.

"Each morning we gather around our queen and kneel before her. We'll pretend I'm the queen. Gather in front of me and kneel."

We all knelt before the teacher sitting on our heels.

"Now raise your arms and repeat after me: 'wattadoe'"

We raised our arms and repeated after the teacher, 'wattadoe' again and again. She explained that 'wattadoe' meant "we bow to you".

The whole class chanted over and over in front of the teacher, with arms held high above their heads: 'wattadoe, wattadoe, wattadoe…"

"Great! Excellent!" the teacher said, now, the next part of the morning ritual, with eyes closed, as you bring your arms down to the ground in front of you and bow to the queen you say 'pyam', which means, "with greatest love"

"Pyam, pyyyyam, pyyyyyam…" the class chanted as we lay prostrate before the teacher.

"Excellent!" she cried. "Now let's put the words together and be island natives sending love to our queen.

The whole class began on their knees, with upraised arms, "wattadoe" and bowed to the ground chanting "pyam" over and over. I felt so proud of myself realizing I had learned something exciting, exotic and new.

Wattadoe... pyam...

Wattadoe ....pyam...

Wattadoe... pyam...

Wattadoe... pyam...

I rhythmically chanted with the class, bowing deeply again and again with eyes closed, and as I did I noticed some of my classmates begin to giggle and thought how rude and disruptive they were

Prostitute To Professor

Wattadoe pyam

Wat a doe pyam

Wat a dope iam

As I chanted more and more kids began to giggle but I was determined to do this right as I continued to put the chants together and do this to the best of my ability

Wat a dope i am

What a dope i am

What a dope i am

And suddenly I heard it. I opened my eyes to find the entire class, teacher included, desperately struggling not to laugh as I bowed deeply again and again, chanting, "what a dope I am".

And I was. I knew it was true. I knew it with all my heart.

But that's another story...

Becca Jacobson MA, M.Ed.

Father/Daughter Lessons

There were six of us after my mom remarried, and it turned out I was the only one who stayed in high school until the end, and when I did, I was 17 and free. There it was, my life before me. Mine to do what I wanted. And what I wanted was money. That's it. That's all I knew. Money was the key to everything and without it, life was unbearable. I knew this because my mom had told me about it all my life. She always carefully reminded us that there wasn't enough money in the house, that we had to stop asking for things and that we had to understand that "money doesn't grow on trees." At the same time, she explained that if you could get money, you could have whatever you wanted. I knew how frustrating it was to not be able to do the things I wanted to do, to not have new clothes to go back to school, to not bother to desire things because they were not going to come. I can hear Mom now, saying, "We can't afford that. We're broke. Always make sure you get money because life is unbearable without it. Money is really hard to get and you should do whatever it takes to get it"... and on and on. I was going to get money.

    I left the small city I had grown up in and moved to Vancouver. My biological dad (or, as I often facetiously - and regrettably- called him, my sperm donor) lived there and he miraculously said I could stay with him for a while. I had a room in his condo, I was in the big city, I could do whatever I wanted, my life was before me, and making money was what mattered.

    Every day, I got the newspaper and looked for work. I knew I could waitress, but I wanted something more. Every day, I saw the same ad: "Exotic dancers wanted - make $500 a week" and every day, I ignored it. But it haunted me. I imagined what I could do with $500 a week. I would be rich!!

    Instead, I answered an ad to get on a team and learn how to earn a commission selling Kirby vacuum cleaners door-to-door. I went to the appointed place and there was a group of men. No women. I did the three week training and learned how to sell door-to-door. I learned to target the elderly, who were lonely and would let you in the door just to have someone to talk to. I learned how to carry that big, bulky vacuum around, bring it into the house, clean part of the living room, talk to the people and tell them how much happier they would be with a Kirby vacuum in their lives.

It was hard work. The team of 5 (4 young men and me, led by our trainer) would get in a van in the morning, load it up with vacuum cleaners, and drive around the city selling. I would be dropped off on a street or trailer park with a partner and told to go to every house on the block. And that was what we did, knocking on door after door, trying to get into the houses. After a couple of weeks, I finally made a sale and earned a $300 commission.

And I kept seeing the other ad in the paper the whole time. That $500 a week was still available.

Then, one day, I showed it to my dad and he said, "Ya, those gals make pretty good money and you could do it. If you want to see what it's like, I'll take you." I felt in that moment almost like we were a father/daughter team and he cared about me; other than letting me stay with him temporarily, it was the only time he had taken me anywhere or done anything with me.

That night, we went to a few local clubs. By then, I was 18 years old and the drinking age was 19, but I got in easily with my dad. I gotta admit, I was a bit shocked watching all those dancers take off everything and at the end of their show, they would roll around on the floor with their legs in the air, showing off everything they had. I mean *everything!* My dad laughed when he saw my face and he said, "Yup, if you're gonna do this, remember, it's not a titty show, it's a clitty show." And that was the only piece of advice my father ever gave me. In later years, I would stop and wonder what could have happened if, at that moment, he had advised me differently.

And so I did it. And I would be an "exotic" dancer on and off for the next 13 years. During that time, I also learned how to make money off-stage. I learned a lot of things. And I tried every drug on the market. And I drank and drank and drank. I went to every party I was ever invited to, including spending more than one weekend with other girls at various Hell's Angels' clubhouses scattered around the city. The Hell's Angels paid you good money if you made yourself available on demand and kept your mouth shut. And that's what I did because I knew it would keep me safe and give me money, drugs and alcohol.

My job gave me the opportunity to travel around, going from town to town for a week at a time, dancing, "partying," and making money. Every now and then some guy would hook me and start a relationship and try to get me to settle down, but it never lasted. And there was that time I got married, but that didn't interrupt my career because my husband liked having an independent wife. Over these 13 years, I would take time off and work for my mom, or hang out for a few months trying to get sober, but I always ended up back at the bars.

And when I came up for air, it was my 31st birthday. I was starting to have more and more trouble getting booked in clubs; there were a lot of 19-year-olds coming up the pike and a 31-year-old who'd been around for over a decade wasn't the first choice.

That's when I started thinking seriously about going to college, which everyone around me thought was hilarious. I'd thought about college since high school, always imagining what it would be like to have a bachelor's degree, but I had never mentioned it. No one in my family was educated and I knew there was no money for college and people in my family didn't go to college.

Sometimes, when I was in the right mood and had drunk too much, I would mention it here and there. "College!" people around me would say, "Who the hell do you think you are? Just get a job in any of the clubs serving drinks; you'll make good tips and a little on the side," and since I was still married, one night after several drinks I even went so far as to dream out loud about one day getting a Ph.D. My husband, who was so amazingly supportive of my stripping and making a little on the side, drew a heavy sigh and very quietly said, "I have no intention of being the doctor's husband."

But I couldn't get the thought out of my head and in 1998,

when I was 32, free from my marriage and my first career and fresh out of my 10th trip to the local detox center, I took my first college course.

But that's another story…

Becca Jacobson MA, M.Ed.

Take-Away: The Joke's On Us

"As you think, so shall you become."

-Bruce Lee-

Everything we experience, everything we have, every person in our lives, every event, our careers, our relationships, EVERYTHING, is a direct result of our thoughts.

This is true and if we could actually realize the significance of it, our whole world would change. Isn't that amazing? In recent years, I really started studying, exploring and practicing this concept in the different forms that I found it expressed by wise people going back centuries. Here are just a few examples:

"The mind is everything, what you think, you become" -

Buddha

"I found that when you start thinking and saying what you really want, then your mind automatically shifts and pulls you in that direction." - Jim Rohn

"Your subconscious mind does not argue with you. It accepts what your conscious mind decrees. If you say, 'I can't afford it,' your subconscious mind works to make it true." - Joseph Murphy

"The empires of the future are the empires of the mind." - Winston Churchill

"When you become the master of your mind, you are master of everything" -Swami Satchitananda

"You must learn a new way to think before you can master a new way to be. - Marianne Williamson

Should I go on? I could, of course, but you get the picture. Great thinkers have been telling us for centuries about the power of our thoughts to mold our lives, but most of us don't hear it. The more I've learned about the power of the mind, the more astonishing it becomes to me. It's one of those things that makes you think, "why doesn't everyone do this?" We've all heard about the importance of our thoughts, but how many of us actually take it seriously? I decided that I would. I made a decision to find out what all the fuss was about and make it my business to put these ideas into practice and prove it to myself once and for all.

Here's what I found.

The joke is on us. All the power we'll ever need to do anything is right between our ears and we either don't believe it or we don't know how to do anything about it. But the real reason, I believe, that most people ignore it is because while changing your thoughts does change your life, it is *a lot of work*.

When I was training to become a coach so I could help others to stay accountable to their dreams, I wanted to make sure I proved the theories by practicing them. I certainly wasn't willing to share my beliefs with others if I wasn't putting them into practice in my own life. So I became my own guinea pig. And I can tell you that changing your thoughts is the hardest work you'll ever do.

And the most rewarding.

How we behave when we're alone matters. The thoughts we entertain in the privacy of our own minds matter. Our private thoughts and actions have a direct effect on our lives, how we are perceived, what comes to us, how successful we are and every other aspect of our lives. Yes, the joke is on us if we think that these things don't matter. In fact, all we have to do is look at a person's life and we can tell what their predominant thought patterns are.

And that's why I emphasized the importance of questioning our beliefs about ourselves and strictly controlling our internal dialogue. Over and over, I see people who casually put themselves down thinking it's somehow okay. It is not okay, not if you want a happy, successful life.

As I mentioned, there are a lot of books on this subject. Have you explored Napoleon Hill? Well, that's just one more example. And they are great books, but I've discovered that most of us don't have the self-discipline to fully implement and follow through on what we read so that we get the results even if we're willing to take on a little hard work. This isn't because we're weak or we don't care. We choose personal development books precisely because we do care but following through on our own is very difficult for many reasons. For starters, we need the motivation and commitment that only comes when others are involved. When I realized this, when I knew I needed more than solitary study, I got myself a coach and joined a community. Now, I've been a member of several communities. They are not all created equal. But I discovered that growing with others often means the difference between success and failure.

Einstein said, ""The world as we have created it is a process of our thinking. It cannot be changed without changing our thinking." Changing our minds, overhauling our thoughts so we can change our lives, takes persistence, commitment, and patience. But it can be done; I've proven it to myself and seen others do it too. And the best time to start, of course, is this very minute. A good start is to write yourself a commitment to pay attention to your internal dialogue. Like everything, this starts with awareness, so commit today to become aware of the messages you're sending to yourself. Then you can begin to change those messages and change your life.

After that, start exploring the literature on this subject. Then, get involved with others who are on the same path.

I have created both a podcast and a community for this very purpose. You already know about the community and you can subscribe to the podcast as well and begin getting short, daily insights for transformative living as I continue to study this subject and bring the findings to you.

https://go.wetransformtogether.com/podcast

Coaching Call! Your Journal

Now that you've got your sacred space, let's talk about journaling. If you're already journaling, congratulations! If not, I hope to convince you to start this practice because it is a powerful way to rewrite your reality. Since your life is nothing more than the way you choose to see it, rewriting your reality (that is, how you see and react to events in your life), is a true paradigm shift.

Here are some guidelines on getting the most out of your journaling practice. You can type, you can write, you can use a pen, pencil, colored pen/pencil. You can write, sketch, doodle or draw. You get to choose! If you're using a doc on your phone/tablet or computer, make sure it's saved somewhere easily accessible. But I recommend a real journal you can hold in your hands, so you're not connected. We want to be journaling without interruptions, or notifications, or the temptation to be distracted. But ultimately, what matters is that you have a journal, it's yours, and you're willing to use it.

Go to your sacred space with your journal. Before you begin, if you are a person who prays, now is a good time to send one up. If prayer is not your path, that's okay. Simply close your eyes, take a few deep breaths, and exhale stress and worries. Your subconscious will respond just the same.

Throughout this book, I'll be giving you specific prompts for your journal, but you can also use it any time you want. Here are some suggested ways:

1. **Reflective Journaling:** Use your journal to reflect on your thoughts, feelings, and experiences. This can help you gain insight into your emotions and personal growth.
2. **Gratitude Journaling**: Each day, write down things you are grateful for. This practice can shift your focus toward positive aspects of your life and foster a sense of appreciation.
3. **Goal Setting:** Use your journal to outline short-term and long-term goals. Break them down into actionable steps, and periodically review and update your progress.

4. **Brain Dumping:** When your mind feels cluttered, do a brain dump in your journal. Write down everything on your mind to clear mental space and organize your thoughts.
5. **Creative Writing**: Explore your creativity by writing short stories, poems, or even starting a novel. Your journal can be a canvas for your imaginative expressions.
6. **Daily Log:** Keep a record of your daily activities, routines, and accomplishments. This can provide a sense of structure and help you identify patterns in your behavior.
7. **Self-Discovery Prompts**: Delve into aspects of yourself you may not have explored. This could include your values, fears, dreams, or personal philosophies.
8. **Quotes Collection:** Jot down quotes or passages from books, articles, or conversations that resonate with you. Reflect on why they resonate and how they apply to your life.
9. **Health and Wellness Tracking:** Monitor your physical and mental well-being. Note your exercise routine, meals, sleep patterns, and any emotional fluctuations to identify trends and make positive adjustments.
10. **Problem Solving:** When facing challenges, use your journal to analyze the situation, brainstorm solutions, and track the outcomes. This can serve as a valuable tool for personal and professional problem-solving.

And that brings us to the question: are you one of the 10% of people who are action-takers? Or, maybe, like me, you're one of the 90% who has decided to join the 10% and find out what it feels like to actually follow through, execute, implement, and get results. You can, you know, any time you choose! It's what I did, and it was, in fact, the game-changer for me. The day I stopped wishing and took action, my life began to change. And, believe me, I was firmly entrenched in the 90% group, as you'll see from my memories.

Well, as we know, inspiration, motivation and solid advice from those who have gone before are all around us in the forms of books, blogs, videos, podcasts and the like, but they're of no real value other than perhaps entertainment unless we get off our butts and put what resonates into action. This alone becomes the major shake-up of our lives. So, if you're a 10 percenter, or have decided to become one, congratulations! That means you'll be with me to the end of this book and taking action as we go.

The Black Out

"Ms. Jacobson, we'd like to offer you the position of English instructor beginning this fall on the condition that you finish your Master's degree before August." In March 2004, when I was 38 and in my last semester at grad school, the phone rang one afternoon about a week after I had interviewed for a position at a small college in another town, and I heard these words.

I was in shock. My entire life flooded before my eyes, every hoot on the pipe, every stag party, every trailer park, every sidewalk, every clubhouse, every man...there were so many men. I heard those people who had told me I was wasting my time. And then I tried to imagine my future self as a community college faculty member with students in my class, with colleagues, with responsibilities, with...respect?

I realized that things like this don't happen every day. I knew that none of the people I had partied with all these years would ever get a good job, let alone one like this. They would never get an education and they would never live on this side of the proverbial tracks. Many of them were dead. Forget the "syndrome," I knew I was a true imposter.

How in the hell was I going to fit in? Grad school had been hard enough, but this? What would I say? How would I become the person that they were offering this job to?

I wasn't sure but I knew for certain that I would have to curb my drinking. I would have to be on my best behavior, indeed, I would have to pretend to be someone else for the rest of my life. It would be years before I realized that I didn't have to pretend, I could become someone else, that, indeed, I was someone else.

What I really ended up doing was living a very unhappy and lonely life for the next 15 years. When I arrived in the new community, one of my first moves was to find a doctor who was loose with her prescription pad. That was actually pretty easy and she supplied me with mild opiates until one of the many addicts she had as patients tried suicide and told the authorities how easy it was to get a prescription from her. I'm guessing that wasn't a fun time in her life. She soon left the community and I had to find a new doctor. That turned out to be a lot more difficult, so, instead, I gave up and turned more heavily to the bottle for escape, which I seemed to need like a drowning person craves air.

These years were reasonably good years punctuated by regular bouts of suffering, struggling, crying, agonizing over the life that was right before me and my inability to grab it. I hid from colleagues, not wanting to make friends and never getting over the feeling of not belonging. I was so afraid they would see through to the "other" me, that I kept to myself as much as possible. I had a job, I got married again, I bought a house, I did my work and every moment that I wasn't working, I drank. I was either working or drinking and it was hell on earth.

Periodically, I would muster up my willpower and make the decision to quit drinking. This was it! No more! I never asked for help. I never did anything different. I just said to myself: I'm done! And that never works. So, I had to endure the agony of trying and failing repeatedly. Each time, it sent me farther into regret and each time, I drank even more afterwards to drown out the stench of failure.

This job included a couple of months off every summer and

I spent the entire time drinking. All my spare time involved alcohol. And as the years rolled by, it got worse and worse. I would drink right up until the day I went back to work and arrived so sick I needed a vacation. I drank every weekend, every holiday, and a lot of evenings. This is not living. This is the height of monotony. I wanted to quit more than anything but I failed every time I tried. I considered killing myself many times.

And then it happened. For years, I had been a black-out drinker. In my younger days, I'd woken up in so many strange places, so many strange beds, with so many strangers, that I'd lost count. So, I was used to blacking out. In fact, at this stage of my life, my goal, when I took my first drink of the day, was not to black out. I think I swore I would only have enough to relax, I wouldn't over do it, but I couldn't quite remember.

In mid-October of 2018, 5 months after my sister's death, I grabbed my bottle after work on my way home for Thanksgiving weekend. Within two hours, I was in a black out. This means, of course, I have no memory of that night, but I do recall vague, dream-like moments of staggering around the house, saying something to my husband.

And then I woke up. I was laying on the couch with my hair matted to my head, my body stunk, my face was dried out and crusty, I was shaking so bad I couldn't pick up the glass of water on the table in front of me, my heart was racing, I was shivering and sweating at the same time. I sat up and saw my husband sitting across the room. "What day is it?" I croaked. I figured I'd better get it together before the weekend ended. "It's Friday," my second husband said, and I was so relieved. I still had the whole weekend to recover! Then he said, "Oct 13th. You haven't been to work, your phone has been ringing, you've been drinking for over a week. I couldn't stop you," he said, "I tried."

My heart burst in my chest and I knew at that moment that my life was over. I had done it. My worst fear had come to pass. I was fired. I was going back to the slums where I belonged. I should have known I couldn't make it in this world. Still, what could I do? I picked up my phone and called my immediate supervisor, who, like me, was a union member, not a manager. I hoped she would advise me.

"Rebecca! We've been worried sick! Are you okay? Where are you?" she asked.

I didn't know what to say, so I stopped trying to think of a lie and just surrendered for the first time in my life: "I need help, it's alcohol." When those words left my lips, I knew I had sealed my fate. All that work, all my education, all of it, was for nothing, I was going back…they were going to send me back where I belonged. And in that moment, I also knew that I deserved it. The whole thing had been a farce. I never should have tried to move outside of the life I was born into. Who the hell did I think I was, anyway?

"You're not coming back," she said, "I know!" I thought, "You don't have to tell me, I know". And then she said, "You're on sick leave. The college will pay, Rebecca, go and get help. I'll get the paperwork from HR today, you just go, find some help and don't come back until you're well."

What? Wait, what did she say?

Ten weeks later, I would return home from the treatment center. Four months later, I would return to work. Not one person would ever speak to me about this episode. And while I was away, I learned that I wasn't a bad person trying to be good. I was a sick person trying to get well.

But that's another story…

The Laughter

When I was about 6 years old in 1971, life was pretty good. My mom was raising me and my brother and sister while she worked at the telephone company giving people information and putting their calls through. We lived in a condo that had a swimming pool. Then, one day, Mom decided she needed help looking after us, so she put an ad in the newspaper for a live-in babysitter. This meant someone we didn't know would actually come and live in our house and start telling us what to do. I was pretty nervous about it all.

But the woman she chose was amazing; her name was Kerry, and she came in tow with a 2-year-old girl named Tish. Kerry told me that she was a lesbian and when I asked her what that was, she just laughed and said it meant she didn't have to deal with men. I didn't care. Turns out my mom didn't care either. In fact, later, I learned that when this woman answered mom's ad and went for an interview, she told my mom straight out: "I'm a lesbian." And my mom said, "I don't care about your personal life as long as you look after my kids."

Kerry taught me a very important lesson. Our condo wasn't far from the river and she told us: "Be careful of the river, stay away because there's a current in it that will drag you to the bottom and kill you." I was confused and terrified and stayed as far away from the river as possible. I imagined a current to be a monster that attacked and killed little kids and I worried that it might be able to get out of the river and come after me. I couldn't understand why the adults in charge of things didn't go in there and get it out. But no one did anything, so I avoided the river obediently. Then one day I asked Mom and Kerry about this and they laughed and laughed.

It turns out that I had a knack for making everyone laugh. Another time we were all riding in the car going somewhere on the highway and I kept seeing signs that said, "Lots for sale." I sat there wondering and wondering, but I stayed quiet. Then I saw another one and another one. Finally, I asked: "Lots of what?" Mom and

Kerry thought that was hilarious and laughed and laughed.

Life was good for a while with Kerry and baby Tish in the house, but it turns out that being a lesbian had its downfalls. Kerry had a few friends come over now and then, but one day she got a special friend, named Wendy, who was at our house a lot. And they like each other so much, that Kerry soon moved out to be with Wendy, took Trish with her and we were alone again. I was sad to see them go.

Then, later on, an opportunity presented itself that got me really excited. In fact, I was surprised at how excited I felt: I could join a softball team! I'd never played on a team, I'd never even played softball before, but the thought really excited me. I imagined myself learning to run, to hit the ball, to be a team player, to get to know the other kids to fit in.

All I had to do was get Mom on board. I planned for days the best way to approach her on this. I knew that money was tight and I needed a baseball glove to join the team. I waited for a day when she was in a good mood. Often, Mom would just be so tired after work that it was best not to talk to her unless I was willing to rub oil on her feet while she snoozed on the couch. That wasn't my favorite job, so I waited for my opportunity and when the time seemed right, I asked. I was in luck. She liked the idea and bought me a beautiful, dark brown mitt that had that unforgettable smell of fresh leather.

I was ready and when the day arrived to show up and join the team, I met the other kids on the field after school. The coach welcomed us all and told us each in turn to say our names and what position we wanted to play.

As he went from kid to kid, I was getting more and more excited. And when my turn came, I said, "I'm Becky, and I want to be the batter."

Everyone laughed and laughed.

The baseball mitt went under my bed and I'm not sure what happened to it after that.

But that's another story…

Cocaine Man vs. The Redneck

"Wake up, Becky, you pissed your pants." How many times that year did I hear these words? How many years afterward did I let them haunt me?

In the spring of 1998, when I was 32 years old, I decided that I was going to pursue my education. I didn't know yet what I wanted to do with my life, but I knew that it would start with a college degree. The year before this, I had survived a one-year crack cocaine binge. I had learned how to smoke the crack pipe and became immediately addicted and obsessed. I loved the feeling it gave me. I wanted to feel like that for the rest of my life. After taking a hit off that pipe, for a fleeting moment, I was free.

And that began the most terrifying year of my life.

The guy who gave me my first hit turned out to be addicted not only to crack but to choking me to unconsciousness. It turned him on. He also loved beating me with his fists, blackening my eyes until they would swell shut. Breaking open my lip until stitches were needed. My face would be so swollen as to be unrecognizable. He threatened to kill my parents, he was going to kidnap my mom's little dog and kill it. He was going to burn down their house. All of this would happen if I tried to leave him, and at the same time, he promised to keep the crack pipe flowing.

He would sit with one leg on either side of my body, his knees on my arms, holding them down and then slowly squeeze my neck until my bladder let go and I lost consciousness. I would slowly regain consciousness with him standing over me, using his foot to shake me, nudging my face, my head, saying, "Wake up, Becky, you pissed your pants..." I'd stagger to the bathroom, wash the blood from my face and clean my body, avoiding the mirror, then stagger back out to the living room looking for the crack pipe, which he always had waiting for me. I'd grab it, inhale as deeply as possible, hold my breath, fall back on the couch and float away on momentary bliss...

I was terrified, I was so trapped and traumatized that I didn't know what to do. I knew that sooner or later, he wouldn't let go of my throat in time and I would not wake up.

It would take days, and weeks for my face to begin to heal, but I knew that sooner or later, it would all happen again. This went on for almost a year and I knew I was going to die. I didn't know what to do about it. I was living in terror. Trapped. I couldn't even believe that this was my life. When my face wasn't bruised, he would send me out to earn some money so we could buy more crack. And on the cycle went. I would ask some of the men I met if they would help me escape but none of them wanted anything to do with it.

Now and then, we would go out to the Indian Reserve, which is what it was called in those days and he would show me his kids. He had three of them with a native woman who had a restraining order against him. He wasn't supposed to be within sight of those kids, let alone their mother, but he would sit there and stare at them for a while, taking hits off his pipe and eventually driving away. Even though I never saw her, I admired that woman for being a survivor.

On and on this went and then one day when he was out, I picked up the phone and called an ex-boyfriend who lived in another city, 8 hours away. In fact, this was the man that I married a few years back and I thought if anyone would help me, it might be him. I told him what was happening and he listened and grunted noncommittally. I hung up. "What can he do," I thought.

Later that night, there came a knock on the door and my heart stopped as cocaine-man went to open it…could it be? And there he was, my husband on paper, a hulking, burly man with a big, untamed beard who worked the oil rigs of Alberta. A "roughneck" and a self-proclaimed "redneck," he stood there snorting like a bull; I swear I saw smoke come out of his nostrils. Somehow, the cocaine man knew that it was all over; he scurried as far from the doorway as he could get in the tiny motel room we called home. At that moment, I saw him for the first time: he was a skinny, pathetic coward who only had courage when he was alone with me and the other women who had had the misfortune to be in his life over the years.

I didn't wait to be told; I was grabbing my stuff as fast as I could while my husband took three strides across the room, stood over the cowering cocaine man, grabbed him by the throat and very, very quietly whispered, "If you ever touch her again, if you go anywhere near her family, I'll come back and happily kill you."

The cocaine man lay cowering in the corner as I finished gathering up my stuff and then me and my husband walked out together, got into his big diesel pick-up and drove away.

I was in shock, torn between the deepest relief I've ever felt and the deepest fear and dread of never having crack cocaine again. I knew that this man wouldn't touch the stuff if his life depended on it; he wouldn't even smoke a joint. He was a beer and vodka man all the way. Part of me wanted to run back. And that part of me scared and shocked me. The other part was trying to figure out what the hell I was going to do with my life now that I had survived my year in hell with cocaine man. I had no money, no job, no home and I was on my way to another province with a guy I was married to on paper only. Luckily, my husband was still an alcoholic, so we were soon drinking and we drank all the way back to his city 8 hours away, which temporarily calmed all these worries.

I never saw cocaine man again, he never approached my parents, and it only took me a few days to forget about doing cocaine. And soon, I would change my life beyond all recognition.

But that's another story…

Take-Away: Carrying Others' Words

"Be careful what you say. You can say something hurtful in ten seconds, but ten years later, the wounds are still there."

-Joel Osteen-

There are many moments in the stories I'm sharing that demonstrate casual words coming from others that had a lasting and profound effect on me. I'm sure, for example, that my mom wouldn't have even remembered calling the 12-year old me a "little slut." Things like this happen to all of us and they can be moments in time that can shape who we are for decades.

If we let them.

What messages are you carrying that were given to you by someone else? It's a fair bet that you've got some belief about yourself that you got from the careless or off-hand remark of another. Words are as dangerous as swords, especially for children. We believe them, and we carry them. They sink deep into our subconscious and actually shape who we become.

We lack confidence and have outbursts of anxiety; we don't even try to accomplish bigger things because we're not intelligent; we resign ourselves to being overweight or unattractive. The list of false beliefs that are given to us is endlessly varied.

And they're not true. They're no more true than the idea that the sun rotates around the earth. They are false. Yes, even yours. But we believe that these false beliefs are actually who we are. They feel like our personality. We say, "I am…" and we believe it.

If we're lucky, some person or event or idea comes from somewhere (perhaps right here!) and causes us to actually stop and ask ourselves: "wait, is that really true? Am I ugly? (or incapable or shy or …)?

Becca Jacobson MA, M.Ed.

The thing about this is that others can see the truth but often we cannot. I have a person in my life right now, for example, who is 30-something and has adopted the notion that they're destined to a life of drudgery. They believe that moving away from making a minimum hourly wage to do something creative and inspiring with their life is not even in the realm of possibility. I can see their intelligence, their potential, and it saddens me when I gently suggest other possibilities and the response is a flat, "I couldn't do that. I don't know how. That's not me." I see wasted potential all around me. And you can see it too.

In others.

What if we decided to stop looking at others' potential and looked at our own regardless of our age, where we've been, what we've done, our level of education or any other "excuse"? Is it possible that you're devaluing yourself in some way?

I encourage you to spend some time with this question. Ask someone you trust about it. And be willing to hear the answer. Great idea, right? Yup, it is, and do you know how many people reading these words will actually do it?

Here we are again at that magic 10% (the truth is that 10% is generous, many argue that this number is much lower).

So if you're in the 10% category, I'm thrilled for you. You'll ask the questions, look in the mirror, and begin to rid yourself of false beliefs. And after that, anything can happen. Congratulations!

And what about the 90%, you ask? That's simple. As you know, I was in this category for over half my life. It's a very comfortable place to be as long as we don't allow ourselves to think too hard about what could have been. We stay where we're comfortable. Young or older, we've closed our minds. We don't change because these ingrained limitations serve us in some way.

If we believe we're stupid, then we can't be expected to succeed, and we don't have to try very hard. If we've been told we're lazy, we have an excuse to be, well, lazy. If we're chronically overweight, it's because that's how we see ourselves. And on and on it goes.

Did you know that you actually have no limitations other than the ones you impose upon yourself? If you don't believe that it's because *you don't want to.* And so the cycle goes.

How to get out of this mess and transform? The fact is that it's incredibly hard to do alone. We just don't see ourselves. So it helps if we have the humility to ask for help, allow someone to help and be willing to hear what they say.

And that, my friend, is more than most of us are willing to do.

But if we will, it becomes quite simple to make the decision to get rid of these false beliefs. And awareness is a solid beginning. So, take some time today and pull out your journal. Ask yourself about this. What nonsense, given to you by someone else, are you allowing? Are you willing to let it go? It starts with a decision followed by patient day-by-day, intentional living. Watch for it, catch it, reverse it with an opposing thought.

And if yours are too deep, get someone to talk it over with. It is worth the effort; after all, it's your life!

Coaching Call! Journaling Opportunity

Congratulations on taking action, on journaling about the ideas you're finding in this book, on subscribing to the podcast and joining the community, on building your sacred space. If you're taking these actions, congratulations are definitely in order. And it's actions like these that will add up to true change in your life.

The beginning of all true change is clarification of what it is that we want. That sounds ridiculously simple, but you'd be surprised how few people actually know what they want. I mean a clear, specific objective in life. This is important because the fact is that if we have a vague idea of what we want, or if we have a bunch of competing desires, we'll get none of them and wonder why our lives are dull, slow, mediocre.

True transformation requires a laser-sharp focus on no more than 3 goals at any one time. Many will say that 5 goals should be our maximum, but I disagree. Focusing on just three goals at a time is transformative for a few reasons:

Increased Focus: When you narrow your goals, you channel your energy and attention into what matters most. This concentrated effort leads to higher quality outcomes.

Enhanced Motivation: Achieving milestones in these three areas provides a motivational boost. Success breeds success, encouraging you to persist.

Manageable Stress: Juggling too many goals can lead to overwhelm. By focusing on three, you maintain enthusiasm and prevent burnout.

So, to begin, in your journal, make a long messy list of everything you'd like to be working on, then narrow it to the top 3 by considering the following.

Reflect on Your Values: Consider what truly matters to you. Your core goals should align with your deepest values, as these are the areas where you'll be most motivated to maintain effort and see results.

Assess Impact: Look at your list and ask, "Which of these

goals will have the most significant positive impact on my life?" The goals with the potential to improve your overall well-being or happiness should rise to the top.

Seek Balance: Aim for goals that touch on different aspects of your life (e.g., health, relationships, personal growth). This holistic approach ensures a well-rounded development.

Be Realistic: Consider your time, resources, and current obligations. It's vital to set goals that are challenging yet achievable to maintain motivation.

Life is unpredictable. Be prepared to reassess and adjust your goals as needed. This isn't about giving up but rather adapting to ensure continued progress towards what truly matters.

By focusing on three main goals, you create a powerful framework for action. This focused approach is more manageable and less overwhelming, allowing for deeper engagement and more significant progress in each area. Remember, it's not about limiting your dreams but rather about optimizing your journey towards them.

The Killer Couch

"I wonder what mood mom is in today?" This was always top of mind during my childhood.

I was 11 when each day the school bus let us off and we walked about a mile home. At this point, my mom had remarried a man with three kids and since she had three, that meant there were now 6 of us. This seemed to make my mom really stressed, more and more with each passing month. The problem was money and trying to look after us all. That was clear. It was very hard to know what to expect when we got home and how mom felt was how we all felt. If she was in her room in "do not disturb" mode, then the house had to be quiet.

If she was feeling energetic, she might have us all run around the house doing chores. She was unpredictable. It wouldn't be until years later that I would learn that she lived with untreated bipolar disorder, depression and addiction. All I knew when I was 11 was that my mom's mood dictated all of our lives, including my stepdad's.

This day, I was the first to walk through the door when we got to the house. I turned from the front door towards the living room and froze, trying to understand what I was seeing. Mom was unconscious, laying back on the couch, one arm flung above her head, the other one buried in piles and piles of bright red paper towels, which were also all around her and spilling onto the floor. One leg was dangling off the couch with the foot on the floor. It took a moment and then my mind computed what I was seeing and I screamed. My older stepbrother came in right behind me and it took him a moment to realize what he was seeing across the room before he grabbed me and pushed me back outside. I was terrified, so confused, so scared for Mom, so lonely imagining life without her. My mind reeled and the afternoon became a blur. The next thing I remember, an ambulance arrived and Mom was taken away. Mom would spend the next 6 weeks in the hospital under observation.

Eight years later, my older sister would land in the same ward with her wrists in bandages and 12 years later, it would be my turn, but those are different stories.

When Mom was gone, stepdad explained everything and I felt much better: Mom had been sitting on the couch and dropped something and as she reached down between the cushions to find it, her wrist was cut by a razor blade that someone had dropped down there who knows when. Wow! I was amazed at how dangerous the living room could be! Yes, I believed this story for a while. Or at least I told myself that I believed it. I wanted to believe it because the alternative was unthinkable.

Even later still, Mom would talk about this incident. She would tell me that she had decided, she couldn't stand living with the burden of debt while trying to raise six kids, so she decided to end it all, but soon afterward changed her mind and called a neighbor to get help. This was a huge mistake. The woman she called barely knew my mom and was delicate and fragile herself. She was the mother of two boys who were in my school and I would later hear from them that my mom had traumatized their mom, who was incapable of helping and had come over to see what the fuss was about and then ran away in fear without calling anyone. She would struggle for years to get over her fright and unsee what she had seen that afternoon in my Mom's living room. We became known as those kids whose Mom had tried to kill herself.

Now, trying to fit in at school, make friends and be somebody became even more difficult. But I tried, in fact, it was my solitary goal in life. Later that year, I took up smoking; soon after I would get drunk for the first time and begin my journey to find the perfect escape. But it all began when I noticed that all the cool kids hung out behind the school and smoked, so I began slinking around trying to become one of them.

At the same time, my sister became cooler and hipper; this was when she got her first bra (so jealous!!) and began getting boyfriends. Not long after this, one of them would spend the weekend at our house and change my life forever and not long after that, my 15-year-old sister would become pregnant by a man of 30 and change all of our lives forever.

But those are other stories…

The Convenient Death

And then, there I was, a 32-year-old undergrad. I didn't mind; I was so serious, so in earnest, so determined to do these 4 years and see my name on a Bachelor's degree that nothing was going to stand in my way. I don't know where this determination came from but it was there and no amount of negative feedback from others, no amount of alcohol and no amount of self-doubt could seem to kill it.

Prostitute To Professor

When I arrived on campus in the fall of 1998, I was fresh out of my 10th trip to the local detox center. They knew me there. I would show up about once a year, sick, shaking and determined to get sober for the last time. I'd stay about a week, eat lots of food, get over the shakes, talk to a couple of counselors, then leave and go back to drinking, usually within a few days or maybe a week or two. There was nothing outside of that center to keep me from drinking, I was lost, had no life that I wanted to claim, couldn't really get any work anymore and was sick to death of selling my body; in fact, by now, I wanted to find a way to never have to be touched by a man again. Drinking killed all of these feelings. But no matter how much I drank, I couldn't kill the desire to do something with my life. In fact, I figured I was born with something odd inside of me. I always wondered: "What's the purpose of all this?" But I hung out with people who thought such questions were inconceivable. They would look at me like I'd asked them the square root of pie. So, I'd have another drink and try to forget about it. But it never died.

So when I actually signed up, some of my family couldn't understand. Some said, "Do you realize you'll be almost 40 when you graduate?" And others, "Do you realize that people with bachelor's degrees work at gas stations." Or, "Do you realize how much student debt you're going to accumulate over 4 years? You'll never pay it off!"

My mom, however, was a different story. She believed in

me. She was still running Gentleman's Escorts, mostly just looking after her own regular clients and she offered to let me live in a condo she owned for cheap rent that I could pay out of my student loans. She sent me food from her organic garden and supported me through encouragement: "You can do this! I'm so proud of you!"

So, I started my journey. I thought the answers I was seeking would be found at college. The fact that I was wrong about that doesn't really matter; getting an education still turned out to be a good idea. For 4 years I studied, drank whenever I could, and drank too much every time, got good grades and in the spring of 2002, graduation day arrived. It was a surprising day; my step-siblings came to congratulate me; just seeing them surprised me because I'd lost touch with them for the most part. And I remember someone taking the time to point out to me how useless a bachelor's degree was. "Really, it's like a high school diploma these days," I was reminded by a person who had no high-school diploma. I was embarrassed by my own ambition, so I just shrugged apologetically and neglected to point out that I was on my way to grad school in the fall but I knew and I was excited as hell.

In the fall of 2002, when I went to the city to go to grad school to get my master's degree, I began seeing my sister because she lived there. One Friday in my 3rd semester, she showed up at my rental with cocaine to entice me to take a break from my studies. When she offered it to me, I was only mildly surprised to discover that I still loved the idea of cocaine. But I was determined never to do it again.

My sister had always known how to get men with money to look after her for more than one night; I never did figure that one out. So I admired her, as she rode around in expensive cars, went on expensive trips and wore expensive clothes but now she was 38, I was 36 and when I started seeing her, I found a different person standing there. I couldn't see what I had admired my whole life. It was gone.

I saw an aging, desperate woman, with inch-long bright red fingernails and 4-inch spiked heels in the afternoon. Another time, she arrived on my doorstep near the university with her store-bought breasts trying to escape as she proceeded to treat me like a 12-year-old. She was still intent on finding her millionaire and she looked at my sweatpants and make-up-free face with despair. I was a grad student trying to fit into a different world at the biggest university in western Canada, and I'm ashamed to say that I just wanted her to go away and leave me alone. But, of course, I didn't. I invited her into my rental and we spent a weekend together getting loaded. It was horrible. She asked, "How can you spend all these years buried in books; do you really think you'll get a job at the end of all this?" I felt massive doubt fill me; she was probably right. I'd be an educated bum paying off student debt for the rest of my life. Yes, it was a horrible weekend.

Becca Jacobson MA, M.Ed.

My sister died in the spring of 2018 by overdosing on fentanyl. I was 53 and she was 55. By that time, I had been a teaching professor for 15 years at a community college. The last time I spoke to her, a couple of weeks earlier, she asked me to send her $15. Yes, $15. I said no. I had sent her thousands of dollars over the years, which had never done her any good. Her response to my no was, "Fine, then I'll just have to sell a couple of ten-dollar blow jobs tonight." With a heavy sigh, I hung up. Of course, I didn't know she would be gone in a few days. She was homeless and living on the street in Vancouver. I knew she wasn't kidding about the blow jobs but I also knew she was manipulating me.

I wanted to rescue her. To go and get her, bring her to my house, give her a home and help her get on her feet, but I also knew that was impossible. And, in fact, that's what her own daughter, whom she'd had when she was 17, did. She couldn't stand her mom living on the street and despite having her own kid, her own husband and her own "normal" life, she had gone to Vancouver and got her mom, found her an apartment and was just about to sacrifice considerable time, money and energy to help her mom, when my sister conveniently died. Even in the end, she somehow still felt like the world owed her something, that men should melt at her feet, that she was above hard work or personal responsibility and that her own daughter ought to sacrifice her happiness to take care of her. Or at least, that's what I thought. Now, I'm not so sure. After all, the timing of my sister's exit from this world was awfully convenient. Now, I like to believe that she made one noble move, for her daughter and grandson, at the very end and got some redemption.

Her death made me excruciatingly sad while, at the same time, it felt like a massive relief.

That's why I couldn't understand why my drinking increased drastically in the months following her death until, in October of 2018, I would hit the worst bottom of my life.

But that's another story…

The Valium Years

"And this one shit herself!" my mom, pointing at me, exclaimed so loud that the entire block could hear. The shame and humiliation I felt in that moment are the only reason I remember this episode so clearly because the truth is, I really can't remember much of growing up. My sister, when we were adults, used to shake her head in amazement when she would reference moments from our childhood that I had no memory of. She would stare at me in awe and ask, "How can you not remember that?" I don't know, but I do know that my childhood consists of about 20 tiny little moments, little vignettes, all of them centered around my single mom and a highly emotional moment in time. And this was one of those moments.

I was 6 or 7, it was the early 1970s, and we were locked out of the house. My sister, my little brother and me and a babysitter who I don't remember at all. I think this was the only time she looked after us. We arrived home after a beautiful afternoon at the park and she discovered that she had left the keys in the house. We lived on a suburban street like a million others with houses that had lawns and backyards. Our backyard ran right up against an apple orchard. The only thing we could do was wait for my mom to get home from work. And this would have been fine except I had to go to the bathroom really bad!

I barely knew this babysitter and I knew she couldn't do anything anyway, so I sat on the curb, held my breath and tried not to move. It was agony and as the moments ticked by it got harder and harder until I couldn't hold it any longer and then I was sitting on the curb in my own mess hoping and praying that no one would come close enough to notice. I just sat there in the deepest shame trying to figure out how I was going to get into the house and cleaned up with no one noticing. I tried to shift my body in such a way as to keep myself away from the mess in my pants. I was getting cold; I could smell myself. I wanted to die. I felt so dirty. The only thing that could make this worse was if anyone else knew about it.

Becca Jacobson MA, M.Ed.

After what felt like hours, my mom's dark green station wagon turned the corner at the end of the street and while I was relieved to know we would soon be in the house, I still hadn't figured out how I was going to get there, into my room for clean clothes, then into the bathroom to clean myself and all of this without anyone noticing. But, it turned out all of these concerns were moot. Before we could go into the house, we had to face Mom's wrath. She was furious when the babysitter told her why we were all loitering outside of the house, why her tea wasn't made, why supper and our homework hadn't been started. Why things weren't the way she expected them to be. Why plans had gone awry, why did she have to arrive home to chaos after a hard day at work?

I sat in my spot, trying to be invisible as she ranted and raved at the top of her lungs, making sure several neighbors came out to see what was going on. My brother and sister stood with their heads down, also trying to be invisible. The babysitter was about 13 and tears poured down her cheeks as my mom made sure she knew how her irresponsibility had destroyed everything. As she yelled and pointed at the babysitter, she paced up and down the lawn and got close enough to me to end her diatribe with, "And this one has shit her pants!" I was a filthy little girl.

Another time, my 7-year-old cousin drowned. I was terrified. It had never occurred to me that kids could die. In fact, until then, I hadn't thought about death at all. And I couldn't stop thinking about it. I got more and more frightened. I began realizing that if my cousin could die, so could my mom, for that matter, so could I! In fact, when I thought this all through to the end, I began to realize that one day I actually would die. We all would. Why? What for? And where would we go? I got so scared as I lay in my bed night after night thinking all of this through. Death. I came to the conclusion that there was no escaping it. And if that was true, then how was I supposed to live? I got more and more confused and terrified until I felt like I couldn't cope with life, I needed to know that I was safe, so I went to my mom in tears.

    She sat with me on the couch and I leaned into her arm, sobbing uncontrollably and trying to tell her about my fears. It was hard. I couldn't come up with the words to describe my deep fear. She just sat there, silent, staring ahead across the room, so I kept sobbing, kept trying to explain how lonely and afraid I felt. I was feeling better as each moment passed, just knowing she was listening to me made everything feel so much better, I felt safer and I felt like maybe I could cope with the world as long as I had her there to look after me. She had a slight smile on her face but her eyes just stared straight across the room as my sobs slowly died and I began to run out of words, so I just sat there sobbing. Then, I could tell that she was going to speak and I looked at her intently, anticipating from her the words that would make it all okay. And she said, "You know, your tears sound like waterfalls. How odd!"

    I was so shocked that my tears dried up immediately. And in that moment, I realized she hadn't heard a word I said. She wasn't there. I don't know where she was but it wasn't there with me and a small part of me began to see that I wasn't really as safe as I had hoped. But the tears dried up and they would be a long time coming again. I learned at that moment how useless they were.

Much, much later I would learn that these were the valium years. My mom, like me, had trouble coping. Perhaps sparked by episodes like the one with the unfortunate babysitter, she had gone to her doctor and told him how hard it was to raise up three kids and hold down a full-time job all by herself, with no child support and her doctor had told her the solution was a prescription for pills. And my mom believed him and she took the pills and she would take them along with stronger and stronger ones until the day she died almost 40 years later.

But that's another story…

Take-Away: Self-sabotage

"And maybe the problem was that there wasn't a problem, and I was just so not used to that, my brain was trying to make one for me. Fuck you, brain."

— Alexis Hall-

If there was an Olympic sport for self-sabotage, I would have a wall lined with gold....how about you? The funny thing about self-sabotage is that I didn't even see it in my life until I actually gave up alcohol. Seriously, I didn't really see drinking as self-sabotage and in fact, it has manifested in way subtler ways than that since I got sober. In other words, look out because it's a sneaky one. In fact, it emerges as a puzzling and counterproductive force. It manifests in various ways, often in behaviors that undermine our own progress and well-being. Whether it's procrastination, self-doubt or engaging in harmful habits, self-sabotage can subtly creep into our lives, hindering our potential for success and happiness. This perplexing phenomenon raises questions about the deeper roots of such counterproductive tendencies and why, at times, we act against our own best interests.

Exploring the underlying causes of self-sabotage reveals a complex interplay of psychological, emotional and behavioral factors. Past traumas, ingrained negative beliefs and fear of success or failure can contribute to self-sabotaging behaviors. These patterns often stem from a lack of self-worth or a deep-seated fear of change. Understanding these roots is crucial for dismantling self-sabotage and paving the way for personal growth and success.

Recognizing self-sabotage in our lives often involves paying attention to recurring behavior and thought patterns that undermine our goals and well-being. It's the procrastination before a crucial deadline, the persistent self-doubt that overshadows achievements or the seemingly inexplicable resistance to positive changes. Catching self-sabotage requires self-awareness, a keen observation of our responses to challenges and an honest evaluation of whether our actions align with our aspirations. It's like spotting a saboteur within, as we notice subtle self-destructive habits or tendencies that hold us back from reaching our full potential. By tuning into these cues, we can take the first step in dismantling self-sabotage and creating a path toward positive transformation.

Now, let's delve into a transformative approach that not only addresses self-sabotage but also empowers us to break free from these patterns and embrace positive change: visualization and using our imagination. In his classic book, "Psycho-Cybernetics," Maxwell Maltz reminds us that our nervous systems and subconscious can't distinguish between imagination and reality. This underscores the power of using our imaginations to visualize ourselves the way we want to be. Of course, it requires consistency.

When we practice visualization, many amazing changes can take place in us. First, we reprogram negative thought patterns. Napoleon Hill said, "Whatever the mind can conceive and believe, the mind can achieve." And there it is. We're done. Go and live that and your life will never be the same…except we're human and we complicate things, forget, disbelieve and otherwise muddle things up. But knowing this and working with it over time can change our lives. And it can begin with visualization, a potent tool for challenging and reshaping negative thought patterns that fuel self-sabotage. By vividly imagining positive outcomes, we can reprogram our minds to focus on success and possibilities.

Visualization also contributes to building confidence and self-efficacy, crucial elements in combating self-sabotage. When we consistently and intentionally visualize our capabilities and success, we strengthen our belief in our ability to overcome challenges, reducing the inclination towards self-sabotaging behaviors.

Visualization serves as a mental rehearsal for success, providing a clear blueprint for achieving goals. We've all heard it before: to achieve our goals, we need a target, something to aim at. Our mental imagery becomes a guide, helping us navigate obstacles and stay on course, countering the tendencies of self-sabotage.

Embracing a positive mindset and visualization aligns us with the principles of the Law of Attraction. Wayne Dyer said, "The law of attraction is this: You don't attract what you want. You attract what you are." And Dr. Ben Hardy said, "Be your future self now." In other words, when we visualize ourselves as we wish to be, doing what we want to do, being successful and reaching our goals, then we will become what we want to become. I spent my life visualizing and expecting failure and I didn't even realize I was doing it. By focusing on positive outcomes, we attract circumstances and opportunities that support our goals, mitigating the impact of self-sabotaging behaviors.

Visualization isn't just a momentary fix; it's a strategy for lasting change. By consistently visualizing positive outcomes, we strengthen our resolve, creating a mindset that actively resists the pull of self-sabotage, leading to sustained personal growth and success.

By integrating these visualization and positive mindset practices into your journey, you're not just addressing self-sabotage;

you're actively cultivating a resilient mindset that propels you toward the life you aspire to live.

And don't worry, you're not alone! Like I said, I won Gold! Even yesterday, I caught myself in a self-sabotaging frame of mind. "Who are you to write a book?" and "You're not really going to tell the world about all the horrible things you've done, are you?!" Luckily, I'm getting pretty good at quickly seeing self-sabotaging thoughts and actions before they can do much damage. But that takes willingness and practice and practice and, to this day, practice. And, as I've said before, it's way easier if you're surrounded by others who are working on it too.

Becca Jacobson MA, M.Ed.

Coaching Call! Find your Tribe Today

Studies consistently show that we cannot thrive in isolation. Trying to change alone is like trying to walk through the park on a treadmill: you're going through the motions, but not getting anywhere. And I know from years of experience just how frustrating that is. I urge you to take action. Write your visualization in your journal and come and learn more about all the concepts in this book directly from me with a group of action-takers.

https://go.wetransformtogether.com/community

The Bathtub Murder

One day in the late 1940s, my mom was walking home from school with her two sisters and her brother. The day was sunny and warm, as it usually was in South Africa. They would go home and play in the yard until dark. They knew better than to disturb their parents, who would be in the house drinking. It's what they did.

Mom didn't care about that; she just wanted her mom to love her. So she tried to be a good girl. It didn't seem to work. Seemed like most times, she irritated her mom no matter what she did but her mom got irritated with everyone, so she tried not to take it personally. She was 8 and one of her favorite things to do was chew on wild parsley that grew underneath a spigot that was constantly dripping. Drip, drip, drip…the water was just enough to keep that little parsley plant alive so mom would go and chew on it. She liked it; besides, there was nothing else to eat after school.

    This day, as they strode towards their tiny house, they saw a big, clean car parked in front of it and wondered who it could be. As they approached the house, a man and woman jumped out of the car, grabbed all four kids, and hustled them into the big car.

    Mom was screaming for her mother and father, but they never came out of the house. The big car drove away with the four siblings and they would never live with their parents again. Apparently, it wasn't safe.

    Instead, the kids were split up. Mom's brother went to an orphanage for boys. And mom's two sisters were sent to another home. She never knew where they went. And mom was taken to an orphanage for girls run by nuns.

    There, she learned to sew, type, and keep her mouth shut. She learned that her parents preferred drinking to parenting and she learned how to live with dozens of other girls in a dormitory.

    And when she was 18, she was given a high school diploma, a little bit of money, a suitcase and was sent out into the world to live her life.

The first thing she did once she found a job was go looking for her parents. She found them drinking in a hotel. They were not interested in her, but she felt a sense of responsibility towards them, so she visited them now and then, brought them food and hoped they would be okay.

Then she got an opportunity to move to London and decided to take it. She had a great job waiting for her in a laboratory that harvested the venom from poisonous snakes to create vaccines. So, off she went to London. Two months later, she got a telegram from her aunt in South Africa telling her that her mother had died and her father was in jail, accused of murdering her.

Mom went home to South Africa to try and help her dad. It turns out that her mom, at 43 years old, died of a heart attack while sitting on the toilet after drinking for 4 days straight without eating. But her dad was in such shock that instead of calling for help, he put her body in the bathtub and sat with her for 3 more days while trying to drink himself to death. It didn't work and on the fourth day, the police were called.

It didn't take them long to figure out that he hadn't murdered her, so he was out of prison by the time Mom got there from London. She said her goodbyes to her Mom. Wishing her dad well, she went back to London because she didn't know what else to do.

And for the rest of her life, she would weep inconsolably on the anniversary of her mother's death. I would try to understand but to me, the incident was so far in the past as to be unimaginable. She would also weep uncontrollably when in certain moods, go into unexpected fits of rage, hide in her room with strict orders not to be disturbed or run around the house cleaning, cooking and whistling. At other times, she would threaten to kill herself or try to kill herself. She would regularly moan about her mom and dad, the nuns, her lost childhood and her "wasted life." She never stopped worrying about money and she made sure we were all aware of how hard it was to look after everyone financially. She would moan about all the horrors she had been through and it wouldn't be until I grew up that I realized that she had lived with untreated depression, bipolar disorder and addiction her entire life.

But that would all come later. When she left South Africa to go back to London, she was 22 years old and when she got there, she would soon meet a young man who was there with the Canadian Navy and he would donate his sperm to my creation and later advise me on career paths. Everything that happened to my mom shaped who she became and she, in turn, shaped who I became.

But those are other stories…

Mother/Daughter Lessons

"But what do I say?" I asked my mom. I was really nervous and didn't want to do what was being asked of me. "Look, it's easy, just say you've got back pain and it's been bothering you for a long time. They can't really tell if you've got back pain and it's quite common. Tell him you need painkillers because you just can't stand it any longer."

With a heavy sigh, I went into the doctor's office for an appointment mom had made for me. The problem was that the doctor knew my mom and wouldn't give her any more pills for two weeks because he'd just given her some a week ago. I knew that I really needed to get those pills for her; she was desperate. So in I went and out I came with a prescription. It was easy.

I was 16 and I learned a lot that day. But the most important thing I learned was how easy it was to lie and how easy it was to get drugs. She even pointed out that you should always be on the lookout for a way to get your doctor's prescription pad when he wasn't looking. Then, you could write your own prescriptions! "Wow," I thought, "that would be cool." And later, I would steal some of my mom's pills and learn that life was a lot easier when you weren't too present. Loved those pills! And I would find ways and means of getting them for many years to come.

In fact, in my early 30s, when I was going to college, the opportunity to grab a prescription pad presented itself. I was at the doctors for something, I can't remember what, but it wasn't pills, and the doctor left the room for a minute and there was his prescription pad. Just sitting there. Before I could think, I grabbed it and tossed it into my purse. He never noticed.

Later that day, I carefully forged myself a prescription for my favorite opiate, went to the pharmacy and handed it to the pharmacist. My heart was throbbing in my chest, my knees were weak, and my ears were ringing as I handed it across the counter and turned to grab a chair and wait. It took them exactly 42 minutes to fill that prescription and every second of it, I was expecting the cops to come through the door. This was a big pharmacy and there were several people working behind the counter. And every time they talked to each other, every time one of them picked up the phone or glanced in my direction, I was sure it was all over.

In those 42 minutes, I thought: "What's wrong with me? I'm in my second year of college and I'm trying to change my life. I'm trying to stay sober. I want a new life. Why am I doing this?" And the answer never came. I know the answer now. I was an addict and that's what addicts do if they try to help themselves. It's not rocket science. In order to change the behavior, I would need a lot of help, a lot of learning about different ways to cope, but that was all so foreign to me that I got no answer to my desperate questions. So I sat there, hoping against hope that they would give me those pills.

And then my name was called and I saw the pharmacist holding a package for me. As I took it from her and paid the bill, I almost fainted with relief. It seemed to take me an hour to walk from the back of the store and out the front doors with my precious package.

And then, within a few days, the pills, like all drugs, were gone and I wanted more, so I pulled out the prescription pad and replayed the episode. This time, I felt much more confident as I wrote myself a prescription and signed the doctor's name, and this time, the police were called.

Maybe because I was going to college, I ended up having to serve community service by giving a local church thrift shop 50 hours of my time over the coming months. The women there knew I was a criminal, but they never asked me what I had done. It was a very awkward 50 hours and no one tried to befriend me.

But that's another story…

The Sober Sunrise

"Some people think they are in community, but they are only in proximity. True community requires commitment and openness."

-David Spangler-

I wish I could say that I came out of that treatment center in 2018 and waltzed off into the sober sunrise, but it wasn't clean and neither was I. The truth of a human experience: life will always be messy, no matter how organized we wish it was.

After 9 weeks in the treatment center, I was set free. It was cold, deep into December. The snow was flying. I was released at 7am, and the winter sun had not yet risen. I knew my exact next steps; I had been planning this day, like someone plotting revenge, for weeks. I had a 6-hour drive home to my husband. He was a beacon, a destination, so I started driving in that direction, carefully watching the clock. With 9 weeks of sobriety, 75 AA meetings, countless counseling sessions, and tons of time to think behind me, I made sure I was parked outside of a liquor store minutes before opening, staring at its glass doors, waiting for them to unlock. I thought of my husband, waiting eagerly at home for my return, hoping that this would be a new beginning for us. No doubt hoping that I would find some happiness. He's a sweet man and my happiness has always been a main focus in his life.

As 8:59 turned to the blessed hour of 9:00am, through the windshield I saw a young woman unlock the doors to the liquor store, and I emerged from my car feeling both defiant and ashamed. It was a small town and people were on their way to work or meeting up at the coffee shop across the street. I tried to be invisible as I bought a bottle of vodka from the woman, "Happy holidays!" she glowed as I walked away, mumbled something back, and bee-lined for my car. I quickly drove away from the bustle and parked on a side street. Tearing the cap off the bottle, I took a deep slug before any thoughts could intervene. I coughed, choked, and gagged, but I got it down, sat back, closed my eyes, and let the heat fill my body. It was an instant familiar relief. I started the car and continued my drive home.

I'm stubborn. I see that now. I've also learned that most people who tend towards addiction are incredibly strong-willed. A double-edged sword which does not help us give up our addictions and also makes us hard to help.

Here's my theory behind why I childishly drove straight to the liquor store that morning (I prefer it to plain stupidity or perverse self-destruction, but, hey, I'm open to suggestions!): I had 9 weeks of sobriety *on someone else's request.* No way. I wasn't going to let anyone tell me what to do. Yes, this is a childish attitude; I see that now, but there it is. So, I had to "prove" that I was in charge of my life and drink.

Pretty absurd. But, what's more important is what I did next, and it is, in my opinion, the key that set me free after over 30 years.

After proving that **I was in charge** by waking up my first morning home with a hangover, I decided to try using the tools I had been given in the rehab center. A novel idea!

I had been welcomed at my first AA meeting when I was in my early 20's, and I flatly refused to be "a joiner." With a total lack of humility, I told myself I could fix myself, I could overcome alcohol, I didn't need them and they had nothing to teach me. I did not believe in community. In fact, I thought it was for weaklings. Here I was in my early 50's with the same community in front of me and something inside of me clicked. "Maybe this could work," I surrendered.

So, I didn't drink that day and went to an AA meeting instead. Then, the next day, I went to another meeting and met a couple of women who took me out for coffee and let me cry. And when I was done, instead of judging me, instead of giving me advice, they told me their own horror stories and I was shocked. They looked so "normal!" That is, I couldn't imagine these two 60+ women, looking for all the world like a couple of librarians, telling me about their own experiences with black outs, with shame, with insanity, and with living sober. That day, I didn't drink. Then, another day passed. And I lived my life in 24-hour blocks from that day 4.5 years ago to this one. While doing that, I strengthened my relationship with God through prayer and meditation. I spent more time with others in sobriety. I started a journaling practice, got a coach, spoke for a while with a counselor, went to more meetings, did some service, did the 12 steps, read a lot of personal development books, found things to do that really excited me and used them to get up each day and not take a drink. But the one thing I stopped doing was this: stubbornly refusing to talk about it and share it. I kept the lines of communication open with others in my life.

One day, not too long after that last drink, I suddenly realized that for the first time in my life, *I had no desire to drink and escape.* I was 54 years old and, after a lifetime, it was gone. Not only that, but I had a community of friends around me that I was growing to love and care about. My life-long, self-imposed solitary confinement had come to an end. I found freedom in being me and watching in amazement when no one told me I didn't belong. I now know that sharing our lives with others is the key to freedom and personal growth, any kind of freedom, any kind of growth. I stood squarely in the middle of reality, seeing the past, excited about the future, and it all felt doable. I could let the past go. I could build something exciting in the future. I wanted to be present. And that's how I feel today: This Becca wants to be aware of each passing moment. She doesn't need to run away anymore.

But that's another story…

Take Away: How to Transform

"If we surround ourselves with people who are successful, who are forward-moving, who are positive, who are focused on producing results, who support us, it will challenge us to be more, do more, and share more."-

Tony Robbins.

Seriously, in the introduction of this book, I mentioned that I was a bit shocked when I sat down and wrote out the memories that I'm sharing with you, especially once they all came together. And I am a bit shocked because I haven't spent my life focused on these events, talking about them, reliving them, or sharing them. In fact, until 5 years ago, I was trying to drink them away. So, seeing them was a bit shocking, not because I was ashamed all over again, and not because I dredged up some new resentments and anger. No, I was shocked because I'm so different from the person in these stories as to feel almost like it wasn't me. And that's a weird feeling.

But the fact is that it actually feels like someone else because it was someone else. Did you know that people change much more than they think they will? Studies on future self psychology show that this is true: we actually do "transform" as we grow. Of course, how much we change depends on several factors and we can definitely speed up the process if we are intentional about it. And, as you know by now, that's what I'm here to encourage you to do: be intentional about getting the changes you want in your life. I'm so different today as to be a completely different person, someone who could not make the choices and decision that the Becky in the stories made. I could not take those actions; indeed, the thought repels me. In other words, yes, we can change, drastically, completely, totally. We can remake our minds, our hearts, our entire psyche.

Did you know that you can change even after years or decades? Well, you can and the way to do it is like many forms of personal development, simple but not easy: make a decision. Make it a priority, not something you might vaguely do in the future. Decide.

If you want a different life, start with a clear vision of the changes you want. We must know exactly what we want; again, it can't be a vague wish. Then you can begin now to behave a little different, think a little different, be a little different. One moment, one day at a time, we can transform ourselves. Of course, you may not want to change everything about yourself, but if something is nagging you, if you don't like, for example, your negative self-talk, make a conscious decision to change it, then work at it day-by-day. If you don't like your tendency to be short tempered, for another example, then get a plan going for that. Or, if you're not satisfied with your position in life, personal or professional, you can change.

Yes, I said this was simple, but not easy. That's because alone you will forget, slip back into your old mental routine. And that's why a small segment of the whole will actually do it. But you can increase your chances by doing it with others, with a coach, a group or both. There is power and magic in this formula. Two or more working together exponentially increase the odds of success. It's a law that some call a "mastermind," some call a "fellowship" and others call a "tribe," but it doesn't matter what you call it, I can attest that it works, and I'm not the only one who knows this. Those who have discovered the power of a community, big or small, working together towards a common goal, will never go back. They know that it's the key to freedom. Yup, humans need each other, like it or not.

And, as my stories show, it was community that saved my life; it was the final catalyst that got me unstuck after over 30 years of trying to fix myself; I finally gave in and the rest just came naturally.

Coaching Call! Get your community now

What have you been trying and struggling to achieve? Have you tried to lose weight over and over? Maybe you just want to get healthier overall. Or maybe your goal is mindset; letting go of false and limiting beliefs. What about goals or habits? Both are tricky. Whatever it is, we know that with a few clicks or taps you'll find amazing advice written by experts. But, will you implement the advice you find? The fact is that alone, we lose motivation, but together, we're unstoppable. The quickest, most effective way to overcome the struggle is to join with others who are also transforming their lives. I urge you to find a community or join mine, but don't struggle alone any more.

Resources

- The "We Transform Together" self-help book study and implementation Academy. Becca spent 20 years working at a college where her job was to help others read, understand, and incorporate into their lives the ideas of great thinkers throughout the ages. And that's what she does now for people like you.

  https://go.wetransformtogether.com/community

- The "We Transform Together" Podcast for daily inspiration to keep on transforming.

  https://go.wetransformtogether.com/podcast

Becca Jacobson MA, M.Ed.

About The Author

Becca Jacobson is not just a master implementation coach; she is a testament to the power of resilience, transformation, and the relentless pursuit of one's dreams. Her journey from a former prostitute to becoming a college professor for 20 years, and now a beacon of hope and change as a coach, is nothing short of inspirational.

This unique path has endowed Prof Becca with an unparalleled depth of empathy and insight into the human spirit's capacity to overcome adversity. She has lived through the very essence of failure and struggle, yet emerged with the conviction that change, though fraught with challenge, is abundantly possible with the right guidance, mindset, and support.

In her current role as a master implementation coach, Prof Becca leverages not only her academic acumen but also her personal experiences of transformation to help others navigate the cluttered landscape of self-help. She understands firsthand that the path to self-improvement is often a labyrinth of confusion and overload, not because of a lack of information but due to an excess of it, and the missing link is often not knowledge, but guidance and action.

Her story is a powerful reminder that no matter where we come from or what we have been through, transformation is within our grasp. Prof Becca embodies the belief that with focus, perseverance, and the right support, anyone can overcome their circumstances and achieve their dreams.

www.ingramcontent.com/pod-product-compliance
Lightning Source LLC
LaVergne TN
LVHW051042011025
822340LV00026B/77